D0965847

This
book belongs
to

_____

_____

a
small child's
Book of Prayers

*To Bernette Ford for her
inspiration and persistence*

—C.S.

Acknowledgments

"Now Another Day Is Breaking" by Ogden Nash. Reprinted from CLASSIC
CHILDREN'S PRAYERS (Word Kids! Word Publishing).
"God Made the Sun" by Leah Gale from PRAYERS FOR CHILDREN.
Copyright © 1942, renewed 1970 by Western Publishing Company Inc.
"Thank God, Who Sends the Gentle Rain" and "God Made the Little Fishes"
from THANK HIM by A.W.I. Chitty. Reprinted with permission of SPCK.
"Thanksgiving" from CHERRY STONES! GARDEN WINGS!
By Ivy O. Eastwick. Copyright © 1962 by Abingdon Press.
Reprinted by permission of Abingdon Press.
"A Child's Grace" by Edith Rutter Leatham (William Collins Sons).

The editors wish to thank Rachel Seed
for her help with this book.

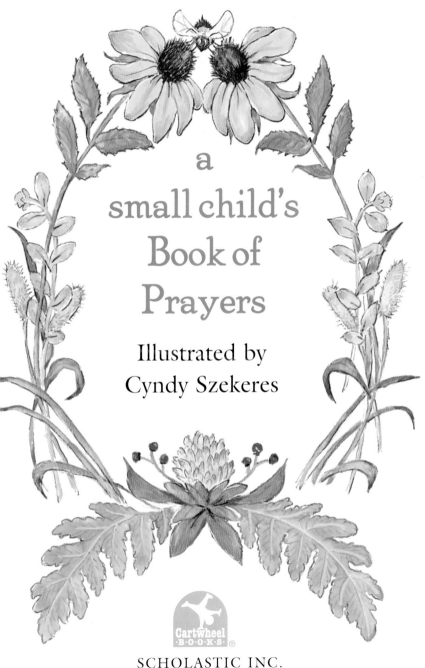

a small child's Book of Prayers

Illustrated by
Cyndy Szekeres

Cartwheel
·B·O·O·K·S·®

SCHOLASTIC INC.
New York   Toronto   London   Auckland   Sydney

Library of Congress Cataloging-in-Publication Data
A small child's book of prayers / compiled and illustrated by Cyndy Szekeres.
p.   cm.
"Cartwheel books."
Summary: A collection of simple prayers for young children, illustrated
with human-like rabbits, mice, cats and other animals.
ISBN 0-590-38363-9
1. Children—Prayer-books and devotions—English. [1. Prayers.]
I. Szekeres, Cyndy.
BV265.S63   1999
242'.82—dc21   98-26478
                                                                  CIP
                                                                  AC

12 11 10 9 8 7 6 5 4 3 2 1   9/9 0/0 01 02 03 04

Printed in Singapore   46
First printing, March 1999

·Contents·

All Things Bright and Beautiful

All things bright and beautiful,
    All creatures great and small,
All things wise and wonderful,
    The Lord God made them all.

Each little flower that opens,
  Each little bird that sings,
He made their glowing colors,
  He made their tiny wings.

The purple-headed mountain,
    The river running by,
The sunset and the morning
    That brightens up the sky;

The cold wind in the winter,
The pleasant summer sun,
The ripe fruits in the garden;
He made them every one.

He gave us eyes to see them,
　And lips that we might tell
How great is God Almighty,
　Who has made all things well.

　　　　　　—*Cecil Frances Alexander*

Now Another Day
Is Breaking

Now another day is breaking,
   Sleep was sweet and so is waking.
Dear Lord, I promised You last night
   Never again to sulk or fight.

Such vows are easier to keep
  When a child is sound asleep.
Today, O Lord, for Your dear sake,
  I'll try to keep them when awake.

—Ogden Nash

We Thank Thee

For mother-love and father-care,
  For brothers strong and sisters fair,
For love at home and here each day,
  For guidance lest we go astray,
Father in Heaven we thank Thee.

For this new morning with its light,
    For rest and shelter of the night,
For health and food and love and friends,
    For every thing His goodness sends,
Father in Heaven, we thank Thee.

—*Ralph Waldo Emerson*

God Made the Sun

God made the sun
　And God made the tree,
God made the mountains
　And God made me.

—*Leah Gale*

God Made the Little Fishes

God made the little fishes,
　The tadpoles and the frogs,
The spiders and the beetles
　We find beneath the logs.
He made the beasties, big and small,
　And He loves them, one and all.

—*A. W. I. Chitty*

Thank God, Who Sends the Gentle Rain

Thank God, who sends the gentle rain
    That thirsty flowers may drink again —
For puddles on the garden path,
    Where little birds may take a bath.

—*A.W. I. Chitty*

Thanksgiving

Thank You for all my hands can hold —
  Apples red and melons gold,
Yellow corn both ripe and sweet,
  Peas and beans so good to eat!

Thank You for all my eyes can see —
Lovely sunlight, field and tree,
White cloud-boats in sea-deep sky,
Soaring bird and butterfly.

Thank You for all my ears can hear —
   Birds' song echoing far and near,
Songs of little stream, big sea,
   Cricket, bullfrog, duck, and bee!

—Ivy O. Eastwick

Dear Father

Dear Father, hear and bless
    Thy beasts and singing birds,
And guard with tenderness
    Small things that have no words.

—Anonymous

A Child's Grace

Thank You for the world so sweet,
Thank You for the food we eat,
Thank You for the birds that sing,
Thank You, God, for everything.

—*Edith Rutter Leatham*

A Prayer

Father, we thank Thee for the night,
  And for the pleasant morning light,
For rest and food and loving care,
  And all that makes the world so fair.

Help us to do the things we should,
  To be to others kind and good,
In all we do, in all we say,
  To grow more loving every day.

—*Anonymous*

Please Give

Please give me what I ask,
  Dear Lord,
If You'd be glad about it.
  But if You think it's
Not for me,
  Please help me do without it.

—*Anonymous*

The Moon

I see the moon,
    And the moon sees me;
God bless the moon,
    And God bless me.

—Anonymous

Prayer For a Child

When it gets dark, the birds and flowers
Shut up their eyes and say good night,
And God who loves them counts the hours,
And keeps them safe till it gets light.

Dear Father, count the hours tonight
   While I'm asleep and cannot see;
And in the morning may the light
   Shine for the birds, the flowers, and me.

                  —*William Hawley Smith*

Now I Lay Me Down To Sleep

Now I lay me down to sleep,
  I pray Thee, Lord, my soul to keep,
Thy love go with me all the night,
  And wake me with the morning light.

—*Anonymous*

Good Night Prayer

Bless my friends, the whole world bless,
   Help me to learn helpfulness;
Keep me ever in Thy sight;
   So to all I say good night.

—*Henry Johnstone*

99/0 1K 3/08

APR 10 2000

BAKER & TAYLOR